THOMAS KINKADE

❧ A CHRISTMAS CELEBRATION ❧

**Andrews McMeel
Publishing**

Kansas City

Thomas Kinkade

❧ A Christmas Celebration ❧

ISBN: 0-7407-3973-5

Library of Congress Control Number: 2003104599

Compiled by Patrick Regan

The most vivid memories of Christmases
past are usually not of gifts given or
received but of the spirit of love, the
special warmth of Christmas worship,
the cherished little habits of home.
–Lois Rand

A family lives in a home, but in a
very real sense the notion of home lives
itself within the family. All the elements
that give life its true richness—love, caring,
support, and even celebrations—are first
found at home among a loving family. At
no time is this more true than at Christmas.

Much of the joy of Christmas comes
from its ability to reconnect us with what
is most important in life. When we
welcome dear friends into our homes, we
revel in their company and catch up on
their lives. When we take heirloom

ornaments out of storage to decorate the tree, we remember Christmases past and all the magic moments wrapped up in them. When we gather to worship, we're reminded once again of the true meaning of Christmas. And when we spend private moments in the intimate company of loved ones, we are reminded that there is nothing quite so important as family.

I hope that the writings and paintings in this collection help reconnect you with the true spirit of Christmas. And I wish you and your family a blessed holiday season.

*From home to home
and heart to heart,
from one place to another,
the warmth and
joy of Christmas
brings us closer to each other.*

Emily Matthews

*Christmas—that magic blanket
that wraps itself about us,
that something so intangible
that it is like a fragrance.*

It may weave a spell of nostalgia.

*Christmas may be a day
of feasting or of prayer,
but always it will be
a day of remembrance—
a day in which we think
of everything we have ever loved.*

Augusta E. Rundel

*For me, the spirit of Christmas
is about letting the loving
but messy little rituals
become just as important
as the solemn and graceful ones.*

It's about making room for everyone.

Ann Michael

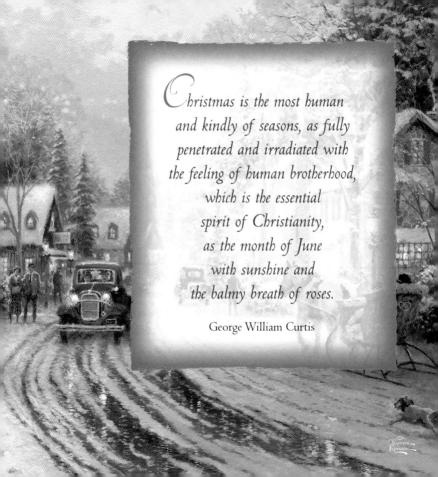

Christmas is the most human and kindly of seasons, as fully penetrated and irradiated with the feeling of human brotherhood, which is the essential spirit of Christianity, as the month of June with sunshine and the balmy breath of roses.

George William Curtis

*It is good to be
children sometimes,
and never better
than at Christmas,
when its mighty Founder
was a child Himself.*

Charles Dickens

*Are you willing to forget
what you have done for other people
and to remember what other people
have done for you; to ignore
what the world owes you
and to think what you owe the world . . .
to close your book of complaints
against the management of the universe
and look around you for a place
where you can sow a few seeds
of happiness—are you willing to do
these things even for a day?
Then you can keep Christmas.*

Henry Van Dyke

*At Christmas
play and make
good cheer,*

*For Christmas comes
but once a year.*

Thomas Tusser

*There is no
ideal Christmas;
only the one Christmas
you decide to make
as a reflection of your
values, desires,
affections, traditions.*

Bill McKibben

*At Christmastime, children play
an essential part in our celebrations.*

*So much of what we do is intended
to please them—and all the
while our hearts keep hearkening
back to the Christmas memories
of our own childhoods.*

*On Christmas Eve, sometimes
we can't help but envy our children
the stars in their eyes, especially
when our own eyes are dull with exhaustion.*

Christmas is so much simpler for a child.

*Can we open our tired
adult eyes to that same simplicity?*

Ellen Sanna

$\mathcal{W}$here we love
is home—
home that our feet
may leave
but not our hearts.

Oliver Wendell Holmes, Sr.

Blessed is the season
which engages
the whole world
in a conspiracy of love.

Hamilton Wright Mabie

*Let us remember that the
Christmas heart is a giving heart,
a wide-open heart that thinks of others first.*

*The birth of the baby Jesus
stands as the most significant
event in all history, because it has meant
the pouring into a sick world
of the healing medicine of love,
which has transformed all manner of hearts
for almost two thousand years. . . .*

*Underneath all the bulging bundles
is this beating Christmas heart.*

George Mathew Adams

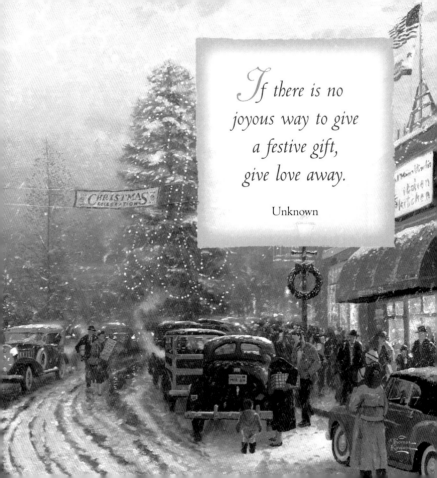

If there is no
joyous way to give
a festive gift,
give love away.

Unknown

*What one loves
in childhood
stays in the heart
forever.*

Mary Jo Putney

A Christmas candle
is a lovely thing;

It makes no noise at all,
But softly gives itself away;

While quite unselfish,
it grows small.

Eva K. Logue

*The rooms were very still
while the pages were
softly turned and the
winter sunshine crept in
to touch the bright heads
and serious faces
with a Christmas greeting.*

Louisa May Alcott

The family is one of nature's masterpieces.

George Santayana

Bless us Lord,
this Christmas,
with quietness
of mind;

Teach us
to be patient
and always
to be kind.

Helen Steiner Rice

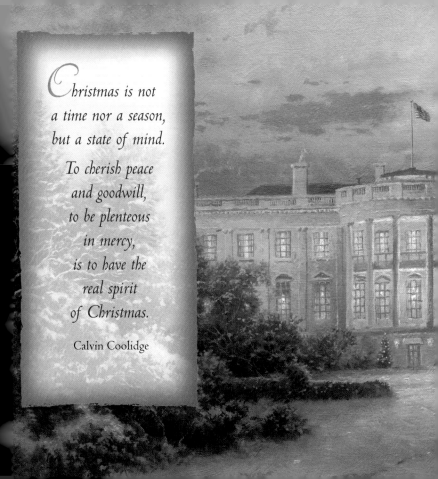

*Christmas is not
a time nor a season,
but a state of mind.*

*To cherish peace
and goodwill,
to be plenteous
in mercy,
is to have the
real spirit
of Christmas.*

Calvin Coolidge

*Christmas Eve was a night
of song that wrapped itself
about you like a shawl.*

*But it warmed more
than your body.*

*It warmed your heart . . .
filled it, too, with melody
that would last forever.*

Bess Streeter Aldrich

*Christmas
is the day
that holds
all time
together.*

Alexander Smith

CHRISTMAS TREE
ANTIQUES

Thomas
Kinkade

*Christmas renews our youth
by stirring our wonder.
The capacity for wonder
has been called our
most pregnant human faculty,
for in it are born our art,
our science, our religion.*

Ralph W. Sockman

Let Us Keep Christmas

Whatever else be lost among the years,

Let us keep Christmas still a shining thing;

Whatever doubts assail us, or what fears,

Let us hold close one day, remembering

Its poignant meaning for the hearts of men.

Let us get back our childlike faith again.

Grace Noll Crowell

*Traditions are
the guideposts driven deep
in our subconscious minds.*

*The most powerful ones
are those we can't
even describe and
aren't even aware of.*

Ellen Goodman

The flow of blessings in our life is directly related to our passing blessings along to someone else.

Thomas Kinkade

$\mathcal{M}$ay you have
the gladness of Christmas
which is hope;

The spirit of Christmas
which is peace;

The heart of Christmas
which is love.

Ada V. Hendricks

What is Christmas?

It is tenderness for the past,
courage for the present,
hope for the future.

It is a fervent wish
that every cup may overflow
with blessings rich and eternal
and that every path
may lead to peace.

Agnes M. Pharo

Every tradition is a collective memory.

Peter L. Berger

Time was with most of us,
when Christmas Day,
encircling all our limited world
like a magic ring, left nothing
out for us to miss or seek;
bound together all our
home enjoyments, affections,
and hopes; grouped everything
and everyone round the
Christmas fire, and made
the little picture shining in our
bright young eyes, complete.

Charles Dickens

*The best things
you can give children,
next to good habits,
are good memories.*

Sydney J. Harris

*Make home
a priority
in life.*

Thomas Kinkade

Holly and Holiness
  Come well together,
Christ-Child and Santa Claus
  Share the white weather;

Plums in plum pudding and
  Turkey with dressing,
Choirs singing Carols—
  All have his blessing.

Ralph W. Seager

*Sometimes we need
to remind ourselves
to relax a little more,
to worry a little less,
to remember the big picture,
and not let the details
overwhelm us.*

Thomas Kinkade

Somehow, not only for Christmas,
But all the long year through,
The joy that you give to others
Is the joy that comes back to you.

And the more you spend in blessing
The poor and lonely and sad,
The more of your heart's possessing
Returns to make you glad.

John Greenleaf Whittier

You give but little when you give of your possessions.

It is when you give of yourself that you truly give.

Kahlil Gibran

Christmas...
is not an external event
at all but a piece
of one's home
that one carries
in one's heart.

Freya Stark